Read
Text Coll

PEARSON

Glenview, Illinois • Boston, Massachusetts • Chandler, Arizona • Hoboken, New Jersey

Cover: Chris Dickason

ISBN-13: 978-0-328-85793-7
ISBN-10:   0-328-85793-9
6 16

Living Together: This Is Home

Eric Carle A House for Hermit Crab

"Time to move," said Hermit Crab one day in January.
"I've grown too big for this little shell."

He had felt safe and snug in his shell. But now it was too snug.
Hermit Crab stepped out of the shell and onto the floor of the ocean.
But it was frightening out in the open sea without a shell to hide in.

"What if a big fish comes along and attacks me?" he thought.
"I must find a new house soon."

7

Early in February, Hermit Crab found just the house he was
looking for. It was a big shell, and strong. He moved right in,
wiggling and waggling about inside it to see how it felt.
It felt just right.

"But it looks so—well, so *plain*," thought Hermit Crab.

8

9

In March, Hermit Crab met some sea anemones.
They swayed gently back and forth in the water.

"How beautiful you are!" said Hermit Crab.
"Would one of you be willing to come and live on my house?
It is so plain, it needs you."

"I'll come," whispered a small sea anemone.

Gently, Hermit Crab picked it up with his claw
and put it on his shell.

12

In April, Hermit Crab passed a flock of starfish moving slowly
along the sea floor.

"How handsome you are!" said Hermit Crab.
"Would one of you be willing to decorate my house?"

"I would," signalled a little sea star.

Carefully, Hermit Crab picked it up with his claw
and put it on his house.

In May, Hermit Crab discovered some coral.
They were hard, and didn't move.

"How pretty you are!" said Hermit Crab.
"Would one of you be willing to help
make my house more beautiful?"

"I would," creaked a crusty coral.

Gingerly, Hermit Crab picked it up with his claw
and placed it on his shell.

In June, Hermit Crab came to a group of snails crawling over
a rock on the ocean floor. They grazed as they went, picking up
algae and bits of debris, and leaving a neat path behind them.

"How tidy and hard-working you are!" said Hermit Crab.
"Would one of you be willing to come and help clean my house?"

"I would," offered one of the snails.

Happily, Hermit Crab picked it up with his claw
and placed it on his shell.

18

In July, Hermit Crab came upon several sea urchins.
They had sharp, prickly needles.

"How fierce you look!" said Hermit Crab.
"Would one of you be willing to protect my house?"

"I would," answered a spiky sea urchin.

Gratefully, Hermit Crab picked it up with his claw
and placed it near his shell.

19

In August, Hermit Crab and his friends wandered into
a forest of seaweed. "It's so dark here," thought Hermit Crab.
"How dim it is," murmured the sea anemone.
"How gloomy it is," whispered the starfish.
"How murky it is," complained the coral.
"I can't see!" said the snail.
"It's like nighttime!" cried the sea urchin.

20

21

In September, Hermit Crab spotted a school of lanternfish
darting through the dark water.

"How bright you are!" said Hermit Crab.
"Would one of you be willing to light up our house?"

"I would," replied one lanternfish. And it swam over near the shell.

In October, Hermit Crab approached a pile of smooth pebbles.

"How sturdy you are!" said Hermit Crab.
"Would you mind if I rearranged you?"

"Not at all," answered the pebbles.

Hermit Crab picked them up one by one with his claw
and built a wall around his shell.

"Now my house is perfect!" cheered Hermit Crab.

But in November, Hermit Crab felt that his shell seemed a bit too small. Little by little, over the year, Hermit Crab had grown. Soon he would have to find another, bigger home.
But he had come to love his friends, the sea anemone, the starfish, the coral, the sea urchin, the snail, the lanternfish, and even the smooth pebbles.

"They have been so good to me," thought Hermit Crab.
"They are like a family. How can I ever leave them?"

27

28

In December, a smaller hermit crab passed by.

"I have outgrown my shell," she said.
"Would you know of a place for me?"

"I have outgrown *my* house, too," answered Hermit Crab.
"I must move on. You are welcome to live here–
 but you must promise to be good to my friends."

"I promise," said the little crab.

29

The following January,
Hermit Crab stepped out and the little crab moved in.

"Couldn't stay in that little shell forever,"
said Hermit Crab as he waved goodbye.

The ocean floor looked wider
than he had remembered,
but Hermit Crab wasn't afraid.

Soon he spied the perfect house–
a big, empty shell. It looked, well,
a little plain, but…

"Sponges!" he thought.
"Barnacles! Clown fish! Sand dollars! Electric eels!
  Oh, there are so many possibilities!
  I can't wait to get started!"

31

.32

A bed for the winter

by Karen Wallace

A fluffy-tailed dormouse
stops by a meadow.

meadow

34

Cold rain is falling.
Soon snow will be coming.

The dormouse is looking
for somewhere to sleep.
She needs a bed for the winter.

A squirrel gathers leaves
high in a tree.
He makes his nest warm
for the cold winter weather.

nest

But a nest in the treetops
is too high for a dormouse.
The dormouse looks up,
then scurries by.

A queen wasp sleeps
under an oak stump.
She has squeezed through
a crack in the rotten wood.

stump

But a crack in an oak stump
is too small for a dormouse.
The dormouse looks in,
then scurries by.

A golden-eyed toad sleeps
under a stone.
It is muddy and wet
and the toad's skin is cold.

But it's too wet for a dormouse
under a stone.
The dormouse looks in,
then scurries by.

A mother brown bear
sleeps in a den.
She is furry and warm.
She stretches and yawns.

den

The dormouse looks in.
The bear's teeth are huge!
The dormouse trembles…
then scurries by.

cave

Bats hang in a cave
and cling to the rock.
They huddle together
and sleep through the winter.

The cave is damp and dark.
It's too cold for a dormouse.
The dormouse looks in,
then scurries by.

A family of rabbits
hop into their burrow.
They live underground
when the weather is cold.
But there are too many rabbits
to make room for a dormouse.

burrow

The dormouse looks in,
then scurries by.

47

An owl
with sharp claws
flies over the meadow.
He is hungry and watchful.
He is hunting for mice.

The owl swoops!
The dormouse
hides in a bush.

Where can she find
a safe bed
for the winter?

The dormouse runs
through the meadow.
Her heart pounds like a drum.
She climbs up a tree trunk.

tree trunk

She crawls into a hole.
She finds a place
that is safe and dry!

Snow falls on the meadow.
The ground is
frozen and hard.
Snug in the tree hole,
the dormouse is sleeping.
Her long, fluffy tail
is wrapped tightly
around her.

Her search is over.
The dormouse is safe.
At last she has found
her bed for the winter!

53

Picture Word List

meadow

page 34

nest

page 37

stump

page 39

den

page 42

cave

page 44

burrow

page 47

tree trunk

page 50

A New Home for Hermit Crab

by Jeanne Bendick art by Diane Blasius

A hermit crab has no shell to protect it. It has big, sharp claws and a hard covering called an exoskeleton on its front, but the rest of its body is soft and unprotected. So the hermit crab lives in empty snail shells.

55

As the hermit crab grows, it has to move into bigger and bigger shells. This crab's old shell is getting too small, so it's looking for a bigger one on the tide pool floor.

This one? The hermit crab rolls a shell over and looks at it. Too small.

That one? It has another hermit crab in it! Sometimes hermit crabs fight each other for a shell. These two have a short claw-pulling match, and then the house-hunting hermit crab moves on.

This one? Just right.
And it's empty. The
hermit crab takes a
quick look around to
be sure there are no
enemies ready to
grab it when it is
unprotected. Then
it jumps out of the old shell,
backs into the new one,

and uses its biggest
claw to close the shell
opening up tight.

Home at last.

Sea Creatures

by Meish Goldish

Come along, come with me,
Take a dive in the deep blue sea.
Put on your gear, let's explore
All the way to the ocean floor!

See that snail wrapped in curls?
Look! An oyster wearing pearls!
Watch the octopus oh so dark,
But don't you dare to pet the shark!

Dive on down, seaward bound,
Motion in the ocean is all around!
Dive on down, seaward bound,
Motion in the ocean is all around!

Now we're very far below,
The lantern fish are all aglow.
Is that a tiny shock you feel?
You just met an electric eel!

Giant blue whales start to stir,
Bigger than dinosaurs ever were!
Wave good-bye to the squid and sponge,
This is the end of our deep-sea plunge!

Dive on down, seaward bound,
Motion in the ocean is all around!
Dive on down, seaward bound,
Motion in the ocean is all around!

Ducks Quack Me Up

by Charles Ghigna

Little duckies in the sun,
I like to see you having fun.
Little duckies on the lake,
I like to hear the noise you make.
Little duckies in a row,
Dinner's waiting just below.
Little duckies, when you sup
You always turn your bottoms up.

Daddy Fell into the Pond
by Alfred Noyes

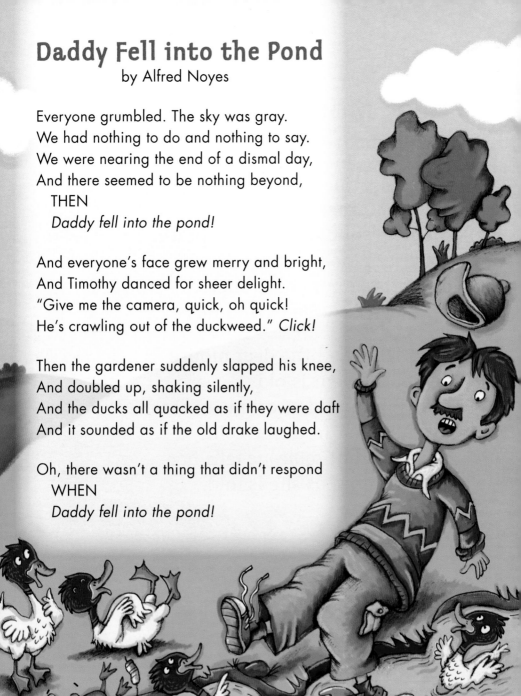

Everyone grumbled. The sky was gray.
We had nothing to do and nothing to say.
We were nearing the end of a dismal day,
And there seemed to be nothing beyond,
 THEN
 Daddy fell into the pond!

And everyone's face grew merry and bright,
And Timothy danced for sheer delight.
"Give me the camera, quick, oh quick!
He's crawling out of the duckweed." *Click!*

Then the gardener suddenly slapped his knee,
And doubled up, shaking silently,
And the ducks all quacked as if they were daft
And it sounded as if the old drake laughed.

Oh, there wasn't a thing that didn't respond
 WHEN
 Daddy fell into the pond!

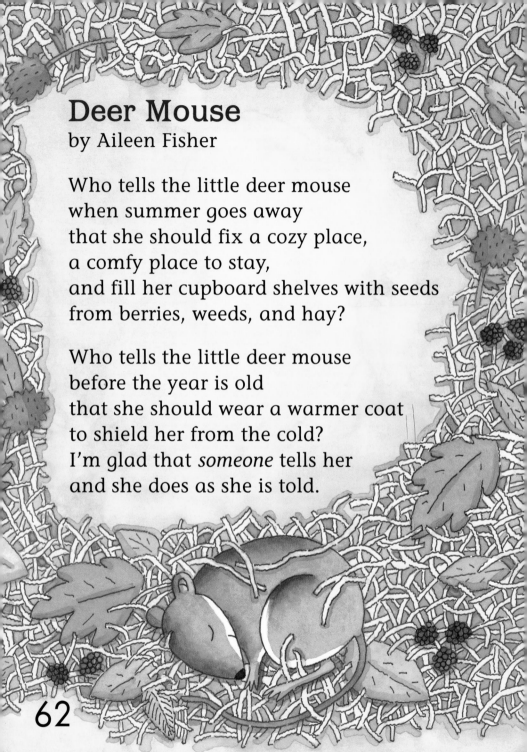

Deer Mouse

by Aileen Fisher

Who tells the little deer mouse
when summer goes away
that she should fix a cozy place,
a comfy place to stay,
and fill her cupboard shelves with seeds
from berries, weeds, and hay?

Who tells the little deer mouse
before the year is old
that she should wear a warmer coat
to shield her from the cold?
I'm glad that *someone* tells her
and she does as she is told.

Text

A House for Hermit Crab, by Eric Carle. Copyright © 1987 by Eric Carle Corporation. Used by permission of Simon & Schuster Books For Young Readers, an imprint of Simon & Schuster Children's Publishing Division. All rights reserved.

Excerpted from *A Bed for the Winter,* by Karen Wallace. Copyright © 2000 by Karen Wallace. Used by permission of Dorling Kindersley, a division of Penguin Group, Inc.

"A New Home for Hermit Crab," from *Exploring an Ocean Tide Pool* by Jeanne Bendick. Copyright © 1992 by Jeanne Bendick. Reprinted by permission of Henry Holt & Company, LLC. All rights reserved. Illustrations copyright © by Diane Blasius.

"Sea Creatures," from *101 Science Poems & Songs for Young Learners* by Meish Goldish. Text copyright © 1996 by Meish Goldish. Reprinted by permission of Scholastic Inc.

"Ducks Quack Me Up," from *Animal Tracks: Wild Poems to Read Aloud,* text by Charles Ghigna, illustrations by John Speirs. Text copyright © 2004 by Charles Ghigna. Illustrations copyright © 2004 by John Speirs. Used by permission of Abrams Books for Young Readers, an imprint of Harry N. Abrams, Inc., New York. All rights reserved.

"Daddy Fell into the Pond," by Alfred Noyes. Used by permission of The Society of Authors as the Literary Representative of the Estate of Alfred Noyes.

"Deer Mouse," from *Cricket in a Thicket* by Aileen Fisher. Copyright © 1965, 1991 by Aileen Fisher. Used by permission of Marian Reiner on behalf of the Boulder Public Library Foundation, Inc.

Illustrations

58–59 Ken Bowser, **61** Hector Borlasca, **62** Bari Weissman

Photographs

Photo locators denoted as follows: Top (T), Center (C), Bottom (B), Left (L), Right (R), Background (Bkgd)

33 (Bkgd) Kotenko Oleksandr/Shutterstock, (T) Julia Zakharova/Shutterstock; **34** (B) Juniors Bildarchiv GmbH/Alamy,(T) Sozaijiten/Pearson Education, Inc.; **36** Juniors Bildarchiv GmbH/Alamy; **37** (B) Juniors Bildarchiv GmbH /Alamy, (T) Dorling Kindersley; **38** David Forster/Alamy; **39** (B) Juniors Bildarchiv GmbH/Alamy,(T) Aopsan/Shutterstock; **40** Ionescu Bogdan/Shutterstock; **41** Mammalpix/Alamy; **42** (B) Breadmaker/Shutterstock, (T) Jeff Gynane/Shutterstock; **43** Juniors Bildarchiv GmbH/Alamy; **44** (T) Meaning/Shutterstock,(inset) Steve Taylor ARPS/Alamy; **45** Mammalpix/Alamy; **46** Dave Bevan/Alamy; **47** (B) Juniors Bildarchiv GmbH/Alamy, (TL) Gilles DeCruyenaere/Shutterstock, (TR) Sally Andrews/ Alamy; **48** Life on White/Alamy; **49** Arterra Picture Library/Alamy; **50** (B) Juniors Bildarchiv GmbH/ Alamy, (T) Reinhold Leitner/Shutterstock; **51** Juniors Bildarchiv GmbH/Alamy; **52** Julia Zakharova/ Shutterstock; **53** Juniors Bildarchiv GmbH /Alamy; **54** (BL) Reinhold Leitner/Shutterstock, (CL) Jeff Gynane/Shutterstock, (C) Steve Taylor ARPS/Alamy, (CR) Sally Andrews/Alamy, (TL) Sozaijiten/Pearson Education, Inc., (TC) Dorling Kindersley, (TR) Aopsan/Shutterstock.